Princess Parrot

by Julie Murray

Abdo
ROYAL ANIMALS
Kids

Abdo Kids Jumbo is an Imprint of Abdo Kids
abdobooks.com

abdobooks.com

Published by Abdo Kids, a division of ABDO, P.O. Box 398166, Minneapolis, Minnesota 55439.

Printed in the United States of America, North Mankato, Minnesota.

102024

012025

THIS BOOK CONTAINS RECYCLED MATERIALS

Photo Credits: Alamy, Shutterstock

Production Contributors: Teddy Borth, Jennie Forsberg, Grace Hansen
Design Contributors: Candice Keimig, Pakou Moua

Library of Congress Control Number: 2024936619

Publisher's Cataloging-in-Publication Data

Names: Murray, Julie, author.

Title: Princess parrot / by Julie Murray

Description: Minneapolis, Minnesota : Abdo Kids, 2025 | Series: Royal animals | Includes online resources and index.

Identifiers: ISBN 9798384903000 (lib. bdg.) | ISBN 9798384903703 (ebook) | ISBN 9798384904052 (Read-to-me ebook)

Subjects: LCSH: Parrots--Juvenile literature. | Birds--Juvenile literature. | Rain forest animals--Juvenile literature. | Animal kingdom--Juvenile literature.

Classification: DDC 598.71--dc23

Table of Contents

Princess Parrot 4

Body 10

Loud Call 16

Food 18

Baby Princess Parrots 20

More Facts 22

Glossary 23

Index 24

Abdo Kids Code 24

Princess Parrot

The princess parrot is found in central and western Australia. It lives in sandy desert areas and grasslands.

Indian Ocean
Australia
Pacific Ocean
N
E
S
W
Princess parrot range

Princess parrots do not stay in one place for too long. They travel throughout the desert in search of rain. They are **rarely** seen in the wild.

The bird's royal name honors Princess Alexandra of Denmark. She became Queen of the United Kingdom in 1901.

United Kingdom
Australia
British Empire 1901
N
S
E
W

Body

The princess parrot is a medium- to large-sized parrot. It is 16 inches (40.6 cm) tall. It has long, **narrow** tail feathers. Males have longer tail feathers than females.

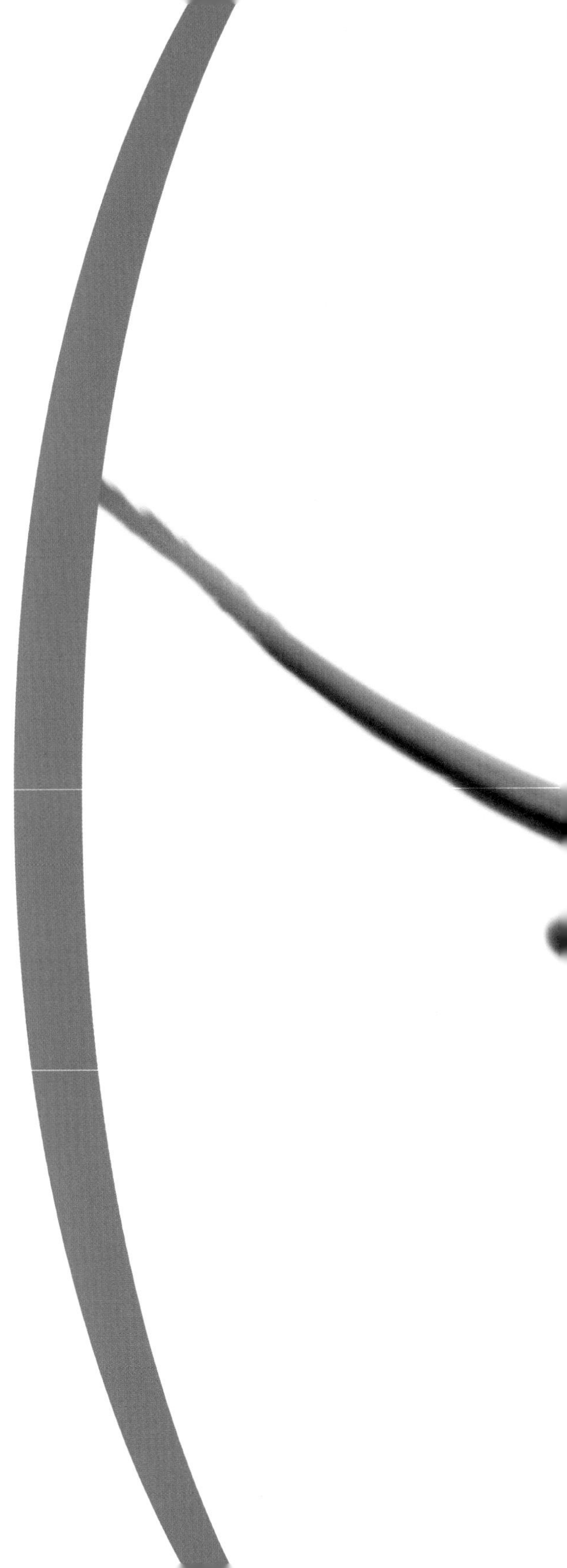

The princess parrot has olive green feathers on its body. It has bright green shoulder patches and a pink throat.

The bird's head is light blue in color. Its beak and eyes are a reddish orange. Males are brighter in color than females.

Loud Call

Princess parrots are known for the loud noises they make. They have many different calls and whistles. They are most active in the morning and at night.

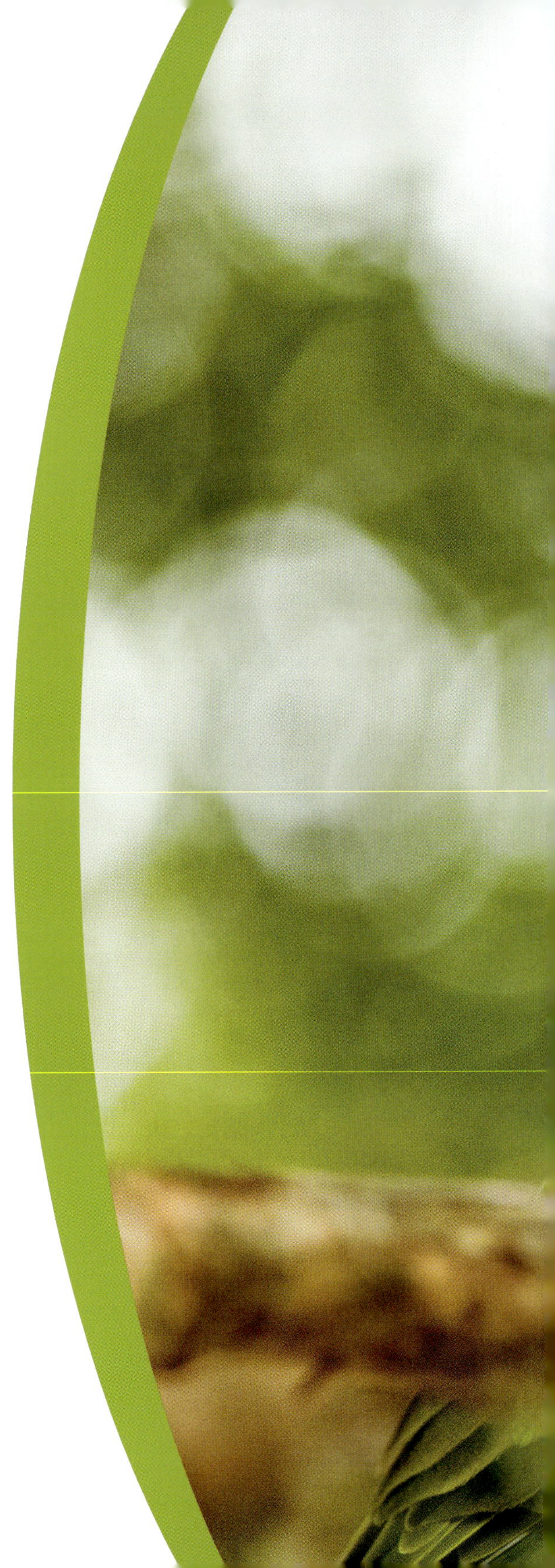

Food

Princess parrots are **herbivores**. They mainly eat seeds and grass. They also eat flowers and fruit.

Baby Princess Parrots

Female princess parrots make nests in **eucalyptus** trees. They lay four to six eggs at a time. Both parents take turns **incubating** the eggs. The eggs hatch about 20 days later.

More Facts

- Princess parrots are popular pets. Their beautiful coloring and ability to **mimic** words make them appealing to bird lovers.

- They go by many names, including Alexandra's parrot, the Queen Alexandra parrot, and the rose-throated parrot.

- Males put on **courtship displays** for females. They fly around a female and bow when they land. Then they ruffle up their head feathers, open their wings, and run back and forth.

Glossary

courtship display – a set of behaviors that animals use to attract a mate and show their desire to have young.

eucalyptus – a kind of tall evergreen tree native to Australia.

herbivore – an animal that only feeds on plants.

incubating – keeping warm until time to hatch.

mimic – to copy or imitate.

narrow – not wide or broad.

rarely – not often.

Index

Alexandra of Denmark 8

Australia 4

beak 14

coloring 12, 14

eggs 20

eyes 14

feathers 10, 12

food 18

habitat 4, 6

habits 6, 16, 20

nest 20

noises 16

range 4

size 10

tail 10

United Kingdom 8